There Is Hope

GW00601013

Lucy Green

Pen Press

With Best Wishes

Lucy Green
x x

First published in Great Britain by Pen Press

All paper used in the printing of this book has been made from
wood grown in managed, sustainable forests.

ISBN13: 978-1-78003-018-0

Printed and bound in the UK
Pen Press is an imprint of Indepenpress Publishing Limited
25 Eastern Place
Brighton
BN2 1GJ

A catalogue record of this book is available from
the British Library

Cover design by Jacqueline Abromeit
Cover photograph 'Sunset over Isle of Wight' by Lucy Green

.

This book is dedicated to:

My Three Special Grandsons

'When you act upon something
you feel you are called to do,
by being in vibrational harmony with it
and by being willing to share it
with as many people as possible
you feel inspired.'

From the Dr. Wayne W Dyer Book - Inspiration

Acknowledgements

I would like to thank my husband, Alan for his support and encouragement.

I would also like to thank two good friends, Annette Leslie and Sallyann Sheridan who started me on my journey of spiritual discovery, and continue to support and believe in me.

Thanks also goes to David Parker, my Tai Chi colleague, for the inspiration behind "The Stationmaster's Daughter."
I am now using this as the title for a story I have begun about my childhood.

Notes on the Author

Overwhelmed with love on the arrival of her grandchildren, Lucy Green often wrote down her feelings on paper. When she lost contact with two of her beloved grandsons, Lucy once again put pen to paper to help deal with her loss. She found herself in a very lonely place and it affected every part of her life. Love, anger, pain and despair are apparent in many of her earlier poems. The loss of her parents and mother-in-law were also experienced in this difficult period.

Moving to the West Country and with the help of like minded friends, came a spiritual awakening, and Lucy has realised that life, now, can only get better.

The resulting poems are here in this book. They offer comfort, hope, and inspiration, with the occasional touch of humour to grandparents who find themselves in similar situations.

There are thousands of grandparents who, having lost contact with their own grandchildren, will understand and identify with Lucy Green's feelings.

To date she still hasn't seen her grandsons, but knows that one day the families will be re-united. She asks for help and guidance every day and sends love to all concerned.

Quote from Times Online—'Almost half (42%) of grandparents lose all contact with their grandchildren after family separation or divorce.'

List of Contents

Grandchildren—The Joy They Bring

To My Grandson

Those chubby hands,
With their little fingers.
The special cuddle,
When the scent of him lingers.
Those great big eyes,
That look into my soul.
The surge of love,
That makes me feel whole.
The laughter, the chuckles.
The chatter, the cries,
Can bring a lump to my throat,
Or tears of joy to my eyes.
A life so precious,
Is my little grandson.
For the rest of my life,
My heart he has won.

Who Can I Be?

What is my title.
Who can I be.
Will it be Grandma,
Or Gran or Nanny.

I ponder, I think.
Must make up my mind.
I will be Nanny.
It makes me sound kind.

Nanny I'll stay,
As long as I can.
Until he is older.
Then I'll become Nan

Second Best Nanny

I know that I am second best.
Son's mothers always are.
Mostly, I ignore it,
Now and then it starts to jar.
When my grandson comes to stay.
He says "I wonder how's my Granny."
I would like to think, when he goes there.
He asks. "How is my Nanny?"

I cook a really lovely meal,
But best cook is still Granny.
I can't compete at mealtimes.
Second best is always Nanny.
I find that I am left behind,
When it comes to babysitting.
Granny lives round the corner.
So to use her is more fitting.

I always live too far away.
Visits few and far between.
And when I ring to have a chat.
Granny has always been.
I know I shouldn't let it.
But it sometimes gets my goat.
Even Grandad can't compete.
The other Grandad's got a boat!

Grandchildren

Another grandchild.
It's a boy!
Another grandchild
Oh, what joy.
Another baby,
To love and cuddle.
Another name,
We must not muddle.
One more child,
In the family.
One more name,
For the family tree.
Babysitting,
Can be a pleasure.
Those moments alone,
We will treasure.
But when we are tired,
And patience we lack.
We know we can always,
Hand them right back!
We now have eight.
And that is just fine.
I'm sure we're not finished.
There still could be nine!

My Grandsons Are Coming

My grandsons are coming.
One's three, and one's five.
With happy smiles and open arms,
They come running up the drive.
These special little boys,
Mean so very much.
'Hello Nanny' they both shout.
And I am always touched.
They laugh, they chatter,
They scrap and they fight.
They love bedtime stories,
And sleep through the night.
When it's time for them to leave.
We have a lovely cuddle.
We blow a kiss and wave goodbye.
Then I clean up all the muddle.

Losing Parents

Please Don't Leave Me

Please don't leave me.
Don't leave me alone.
I am struggling to cope,
Now my father has gone.

I need to be strong,
For my brother and Mum.
But who will console me,
As I am left numb.

The man I looked up to,
Has left me behind
He was loved and admired,
Special and kind.

Alas I just know,
The only one there for me.
The one now who's constant.
That person is me.

No-one Asks

A while ago, my father died.
And people said to me.
"How is your mother coping?"
No-one asked how I felt.
No-one asked about me.

My mother-in-law has passed away.
And people say to me.
"How is your husband coping?"
No-one asks how I feel.
No-one asks about me.

My mother now has cancer.
And people say to me.
"How is your brother coping?"
No-one asks how I feel.
No-one asks about me.

One by one they are leaving.
And I am left, but you see.
No-one asks how I cope.
No-one asks how I feel.
No-one asks about me.

Sick Mums

Life with the Mums is difficult.
And gets harder all the time.
Your Mum is losing her memory.
The one with cancer is mine.
Neither will get better.
We both accept their fate.
Trying to do things for them.
Before it is too late.
Neither of us have been too close,
To these Mums of ours.
And at times, we can resent,
The demands upon our hours.
You are just an only child.
Pressure on you never ends.
I am not an only child,
But on me my mother depends.
We will give the help we can
And when they are at rest.
We can both look back and say,
We did our very best.

Cemetery

Names long forgotten.
They lie sleeping.
Above, silent stones,
Their vigil are keeping.

Resting places.
Many neglected.
Some with no name.
The world has rejected.

Nothing moves.
Nothing is heard.
Except the song
Of a solitary bird.

Everywhere so still.
They peacefully lie.
Wind through the trees,
Does gently sigh.

How Are You?

"Hello" they say,
"How are you?"
"OK," we reply.
"And you too?"

But do we really care.
Do we want to know.
Other people's problems.
As on our way we go.

People always say they're fine.
But often it's not right.
How often do we tell the truth.
We're just being polite.

No-one really wants to hear,
Our troubles and our strife.
All we ever want to do,
Is get on with our life.

Next time when you ask someone,
How are they today.
Listen much more carefully,
To what they really want to say.

Loss Of Contact With Grandsons

Son, Daughter-In-Law

Son, daughter-in-law,
Don't you care.
Think of us for once,
If you dare.

While you quarrel,
And make a fuss.
You give no heed,
To the likes of us.

Children, grandparents.
Not kept in the know.
While all that anger,
Flies to and fro.

We wait the outcome.
It's really so sad.
We've now lost all contact
That we ever had.

Sudden Realisation

Sudden realisation.
Nothing will be the same.
What is happening to us?
They are the ones to blame.
Her father and her mother,
Prop her up with their support.
While we stand alone, confused.
Outside the door of the court.
Her tales of life with our son,
Have cut us to the core.
She lives in a world of fantasy.
Points, she continues to score.
The courtroom with its judge.
Sits there in all its glory.
Listening to the words,
Of a very different story.
They say she is a good mother.
They are always taken in.
By her beguiling nature.
Her pretty face, her grin.
So here we stand defeated.
She has won again.
The court is no supporter,
Of a son who is in pain.
There's no point in trying,
To change the judge's mind.
It's all in favour of the Mum.
But a better Dad you'll never find.

Distant Grandsons

I would love to see my grandsons,
Before they get much older.
But their mother says I cannot.
She couldn't be any colder.

My son and her have parted,
And she's taken them away.
She's now with a new man.
With him they'll have to stay.

She tells the boys who they can see,
And it really is so sad.
Their new life is much better.
She has no time for their Dad.

He has been fighting, tooth and nail,
To get to see his boys.
But their birthdays come and go,
They are not allowed our toys.

One day I'll see my grandsons.
I hope it won't be long.
Then maybe between us all,
We'll put right all the wrong.

Anger So Deep

Anger so deep,
It gnaws you inside.
Rage bubbling up.
Not easy to hide.
Why does she do it.
What's her intent.
To destroy our family.
She's always hell bent.

With parents' support,
Her acts are so callous.
The children are pawns.
She uses to taunt us.
Revenge is so sweet.
I sit here and plan it.
But that's not the answer.
I know, but can't help it.

One day I might,
Learn to forgive.
I hope with herself,
She is able to live.
The system is useless.
It happens to others.
Courts and judges are blind,
To these vengeful mothers.

Searching

Searching.
Through all the trouble and strife.
Searching.
For the meaning of life.
Searching.
For something I cannot find.
Searching.
For some peace of mind.
Searching
For love, happiness or wealth.
Searching.
For the best of health.
Searching.
What am I searching for?
Searching.
Will I search for ever more?
Searching.
For I know not what.
Searching.
For something I haven't got.

Is It Me?

I have a husband who loves me in his way.
Is it me?
I have sons I am proud of, but partners come first.
Is it me?
I have grandchildren, two I can't see.
Is it me?
I have a lovely home, but not where I want to live.
Is it me?
I have a beautiful garden, but can't see the outside
world.
Is it me?
I have a job I enjoy, but don't work for myself.
Is it me?
I have security, but worry about the future.
Is it me?
I have so many things to be thankful for,
But there must be something missing.
Is it me?
It must be me.

People Just Don't Know

People just don't know,
Exactly how I feel.
To them it's not a problem,
But to me it's very real.

If they were in my shoes.
Is a comment that I hear.
They might understand me.
It might become more clear.

But they will never be,
So will never know for sure.
The mixed emotions that I feel.
Or the pain that I endure.

What Am I Doing?

What am I doing?
What do I want?
Where on earth do I go?
I am confused.
Can't make up my mind.
I really just don't know.

I want to get out.
I want to be free.
I want to leave.
I want to be me.

Sleep

Sleep, Oh sleep.
Evading me, taunting me.
Holding me in your power.

The long dark night.
Thoughts in turmoil.
Hour after lonely hour.

Sleep, Oh sleep.
Will you ever come.
And take this dread away.

Of lying here,
With tormented mind.
Until the break of day.

My Pets

Dogs Are My Saviours

Dogs are my saviours.
My life they enhance.
Their friendly faces.
I see at a glance.

They gaze at me,
With adoring eyes.
They don't desert me.
Don't fool me with lies.

My dogs are constant,
Whatever becomes.
When I'm deserted.
When I am left numb.

My Dogs

My dogs are only mongrels.
Which matters not to me.
I couldn't love them any more.
If they were pedigree.
They love me unconditionally.
No matter what I've done.
Always there to make me smile,
Whenever I am down.
They always want to go for walks,
Up to the nearest park.
I only have to think we'll go,
And they begin to bark.
They can see into my mind,
And know exactly what I think.
They must be telepathic.
Between us there's a link.
My dogs are only mongrels,
But I need them in my life.
To lose one of my faithful friends,
Would cut me like a knife.

My Dog Alone

My dog alone.
A lonely soul.
My dog alone.
Now there's a hole.
She had a pal,
But now she's gone.
My dog alone.
But life goes on.

She needs a friend,
And so do I.
Another pal,
I'll have to buy.
A visit I'll make,
To the nearest home.
For another lonely soul,
In need of a home.

Work Related Poems

The Drive To Work

I am on my way to work,
And the skyline is so hazy.
I would really rather be,
On that hill, feeling lazy.

The sky above a perfect blue.
The skylark soaring high.
The sun a giant yellow ball,
As I go driving by.

Now I'm in a traffic jam.
Waiting for the light.
Nearly at my place of work.
Where I will stay 'til night.

Tomorrow I will do the same.
And the day after too.
Every day I drive to work.
In the sunshine, in the queue.

The View From My Window

The view from my window,
Is restricted by the bars.
Leaded glass, so I am told.
Can only just see the cars.
The traffic either races past,
Or drops down to a crawl.
Depending on the time of day,
Or if traffic lights catch all.
The buses I can see much better,
And the passengers inside.
They don't know that they are watched,
As in my room I hide.
Across the road there is a Home,
For all the elderly.
I catch a glimpse of one or two,
But I know they don't see me.
The trees sway gently in the breeze.
The sun is shining too.
I can see a cloudless sky,
But it's me who feels so blue.
There is another world out there,
And I wish that I could go,
But I am here 'til evening time,
As I look through my window.

A Home From Home

A home from home.
The advert will say.
Everyone is happy.
You will enjoy your stay.
A very old lady arrives,
With knuckles that are bent.
Then someone with a walking stick.
It is an elderly gent.
Newcomers always nervous,
And feeling rather sad.
They will miss their homes,
And the freedom that they had.
Residents have their own rooms.
Or, if they want, can share.
Allowed to bring belongings,
So the room is not so bare.
Breakfast now is over,
And they all sit down to wait.
Lunchtime in three hours.
Hope that it's not late.
It's afternoon and Matron calls -
"It's Bingo time, come play."
A home from home, I don't think so.
Oh well, tomorrow's another day.

Foggy Day

It is foggy.
I can't see.
In all the world.
There's only me.

No hills, no trees,
No sun, no sky.
Only the fog.
As I drive by.

Just for a while.
I'm all alone,
And I can't wait,
To get back home.

But, wait a minute.
Now I can see.
Thank goodness for that.
There isn't just me.

Receptionists

Every day we sit here.
Seeing clients come and go.
Trying to keep busy.
But time goes by so slow.

Answering the telephone.
Always friendly and polite.
Keeping track of everyone.
Making sure they are alright.

Doctors want the diary full.
Clients want to pay.
We are always making dates,
For many months away.

See you in six months,
Calls an over cheerful soul.
Six months! I don't think so.
Escaping is our goal!

Spiritual Awakening

This Little House

Somewhere safe.
A little retreat.
Time to think.
A chance to meet.
My Spirit, my inspiration.
Meditating, visualising.
Positive thoughts,
Tai chi, exercising.
All these things,
I needed to do.
To restart my life,
And begin anew.
This little house,
Has been my home.
But now I am healed.
I am ready to roam.
This special place,
Has been such a treasure.
Giving me strength and support,
In equal measure.

Onwards With My Source

Onwards with my Source.
In our world together now.
With faith and trust,
To his wisdom I'll bow.
We'll walk side by side,
On this path of life.
With positive thoughts.
No more trouble or strife.
An end to conflict,
And mis-trust of course.
The rest of my life,
Spent in joy with my Source.

My Spirit Guide

When I now need answers,
Spirit comes to my aid.
He's always there to help me.
I no longer feel afraid.
When ever I have questions.
To my Spirit I will speak.
He will always guide me,
To the answers that I seek.
The answers are not always,
There in black and white.
But I am given choices,
And I choose which I think right.
The signs are always there,
For which route that I must take.
But I know I will be guided,
To the decisions I must make.

Compassion

Anger has turned to compassion,
And caring for all those involved.
I now see, when anger breeds anger,
Problems can never be solved.

There are always two sides to a story,
And when we watch from the sideline,
Between what is and what isn't,
Can be a very fine line.

I care about all those concerned,
And want to make everything right.
Those two boys are what is important.
And so to that end I will fight.

There Is Hope

There is hope at the end of the tunnel.
A feeling of strong belief.
There is light at the end of the tunnel.
Bringing a sense of relief.
Years of sadness and despair,
With no hope at all.
Are changing to a lightness of heart.
Waiting for the call.

There is hope at the end of the tunnel.
I feel it in my heart.
There is light at the end of the tunnel.
Bringing a brand new start.
We can now begin again.
And forget all the past.
The time is coming very soon.
The good times now will last

Laughter And Cuddles

Ryans's laughter,
And Charlie's cuddles.
Always fresh in my mind.
Though it is years,
Since I have felt,
Anything of this kind.

I know in my heart,
When all is settled,
And we are together once more.
Nothing and no-one,
Will keep us apart.
Laughter and cuddles galore.

Positive Thinking

I feel so much more positive.
Always think good thoughts.
Sending them over the air waves.
Hoping they will be caught.

One day my positive thinking,
Will reach its destination.
Then everything will be alright.
No more hesitation.

We will all meet up again.
And all talk to one another.
Friendly faces all around.
Brother meeting brother.

My Grandsons

I now know that I will see,
My grandsons once again.
As they get older, they will know,
The anguish and the pain,
That has been caused.
Years passing by,
With never a word.
No! time doesn't fly.

One day they will be grown up.
With children of their own.
Then perhaps they'll understand,
What it's like to be alone.
When they come to visit.
When I see their face.
Then everything I've wished for,
Will all fall into place.

Inspiration From The Sea

My Dream

My lifelong dream will always be,
To live beside the sea.
To see the waves come crashing in,
Will be pure heaven for me.
Every day to wake up,
And go outside the door,
And know that I am by the sea.
I can ask no more.
Ever changing seasons.
Always something new.
The shifting sands, the endless sea.
Every day a different view.

Every summer I can sit,
Alone upon the sand.
Just me alone with all my thoughts.
Sand trickling through my hand.
Every winter I can walk,
Along the cliffs so steep.
The winds will howl around me,
My balance hard to keep.
Golden autumn, cheerful spring.
Each day a different scene.
I will thank my lucky stars.
That I achieved my dream.

Ebb And Flow

Ebb and flow, ebb and flow.
Always moving to and fro.
Tide creeping in, then out again.
Sand gently moving grain by grain.
Tide angry, rushing up the beach.
White foam rising as rocks they reach.

Seaweed, stones, pebbles and shells,
All are washed up, carried by swells.
Seagulls swoop and try to land,
On the water or on the sand.
Everlasting ebb and flow.
Always moving to and fro.

Tide Coming In

Sky bright blue.
An occasional cloud.
Tide creeping in.
Waves getting loud.
Seagulls circling.
While children play.
Parents are lazing.
They're here for the day.

Tide coming in,
First slowly, then rushing.
Moves up the beach.
Over rocks, gushing.
Creeps up behind you,
Without any warning.
You must be careful.
This bright sunny morning.

A Man In A Yacht

A man in a yacht,
Out in the bay.
What is he doing,
On this very still day.
No wind for his sails.
No current to guide.
Is he there for the peace,
While his time he bides.
Does he need time,
To think and to plan.
What to do with his life.
This solitary man.
Or does he just fish,
With his rod and his line.
Enjoying himself,
'til he heads back to Lyme

Holidays

Ocean glistening.
Silhouettes on sand.
Strolling along.
Hand held in hand.
From the shade,
Of my straw thatched cover,
I people watch.
Is that friend or lover?
Bikinis that large,
Should not be allowed.
And who are they,
That noisy crowd.
Smell of sun cream.
And all about,
Glistening bodies,
Lying stretched out.
All determined,
To soak up the rays.
Making the most,
Of their holidays.

Inspiration From The Countryside

The Call Of The Curlew

The call of the curlew.
That wonderful sound.
Invokes the best memories,
That I've ever found.
Early morning, or evening time,
Out on the mud flats,
That familiar line.
Curlew, curlew.
Their voices do carry.
While across the river,
To listen, I'll tarry.
Then nightfall arrives,
And they sleep safe and warm.
Tomorrow, they'll rise,
And call again, come the dawn.

Birds

Birds outside my window.
They come in ones and twos.
With seed and oats and crumbs of bread.
They don't know which to choose.

Birds outside my window.
They come in fours and fives.
The weather is so cold.
We must keep them alive.

Birds outside my window.
They come in eights and nines.
Plenty of food at this house.
There must be a café sign.

Birds outside my window.
So many different sorts.
I really can't imagine,
How much food I've bought.

Birds outside my window.
They eat and drink and play.
They bring me so much pleasure.
I could sit and watch all day.

Whose Woods?

Whose woods are these?
I think I know.
Elves and fairies,
Of long ago.
The tall straight trees,
With their canopy of leaves.
The bushes below,
Where spiders they weave,
Their webs of silky thread so fine.
Where raindrops collect on leaves that shine.
If you stand amidst the silence,
And listen carefully.
The elves and fairies can still be heard.
Voices calling, playfully.

Clouds

Dark, foreboding, menacing clouds.
Black as thunder, hanging so low,
I could reach out and touch.
Push them away, make them go.

White, fluffy, cotton wool clouds.
Floating in a heavenly blue sky.
Far above and out of my reach.
To touch them I'd need to fly.

Rainbow

The storm has passed,
Now only clouds.
I feel the calm.
I speak out loud.
"What are these shades,
Of blue and green.
Hues so bright,
They draw me in."
I stand in awe,
At that great arc.
Rays so clear,
Against the dark.
All the pains of the world seem small,
When this view holds me in thrall.

Thunder And Lightning

Lightning flashing.
Thunder rolling.
People dashing,
Instead of strolling.
Diving for shelter,
Under a cover.
Hoping the storm,
Will soon pass over.
Rain lashing down,
Flooding the drains.
The weather's all wrong.
Shouldn't be rain.
Suddenly it's over.
The storm moves away.
Out people come,
To enjoy the day.

Two Paths

The path that I trod,
As I wended my way.
Was beset with problems,
That filled my day.
Noisy, chaotic.
Desperate for peace.
Where was the end.
Would it never cease.

The path I now tread,
Is surrounded by trees.
Ferns and grasses,
Caress my bare knees.
Peaceful, tranquil.
No sound to be heard,
But the buzzing of bees.
And the song of a bird.

Miscellaneous Subjects

An Eye For An Eye

Pain and anger.
Disgust and outrage.
"Kill him," you shout.
"That beast in a cage.
Get rid of him."
I hear you cry.
A tooth for a tooth.
An eye for an eye.
He is evil.
He must go.
Something painful.
Something slow.
But could you do it?
The drug or the knot?
Could you do it
I know I could not.
You'd be no better.
You'd be to blame.
An eye for an eye.
Exactly the same.
Why not leave him,
Alone on the shelf.
Or give him the means.
Let him do it himself.

Celebrity

I have made it, I've arrived.
It's wonderful to be alive.
I walk around, my head in the air.
While everybody turns to stare.
They greet me with smiles, they shake my hand.
How I love to be a celebrity in this land.

But wait, it's gone, my privacy.
My whole life invaded, utter lunacy.
I have no peace, no time to myself.
I must be on show, or get left on the shelf.
Too much pressure, it's got out of hand.
How I hate to be a celebrity in this land.

The Stationmaster's Daughter

I was the Stationmaster's daughter.
A privileged place to be.
Childhood was a special time.
With adventures galore for me.

The platform was my playground.
The signal box my den.
The station always quiet.
Trains only now and then.

As stationmaster's daughter,
Nothing was out of bounds.
So I was always popular,
With playmates calling round.

Riding on the engines.
Moving trucks around.
Unloading in the grain store.
Hiding places found.

Long days in the sunshine.
Never without a friend.
I was the Stationmaster's daughter,
Hoping it would never end.

Light Hearted And Humorous

Losing Weight

I'm losing weight thank goodness.
I really was depressed.
Nothing fitted properly,
Whenever I got dressed.
Skirts with too tight waistband.
Not one spare tyre, but two!
Trousers so tight I split the seam.
My mood was very blue.
I couldn't open my wardrobe door,
And choose what I would wear.
I had to wear what fitted me,
And leave the nice clothes there.
Now that I have found the way,
With my new eating plan.
It is so easy to lose weight.
I am confident I can.
Already one stone lighter.
And one spare tyre has gone.
With one more stone to go,
It shouldn't take too long.
I'm losing weight thank goodness.
Soon be back to my old self.
Wearing all my lovely clothes,
That sit there on the shelf.

The Real Me

At last I've found the real me,
Hidden under all the weight.
I'm now back to where I was.
And I really do feel great.

No more buying clothes to cover.
No more feeling fat.
I can look at all my clothes.
And today say, "I'll wear that."

I Know A Little Elephant

I know a little elephant,
And her name is Ellie.
She likes buns and cakes and sweets,
But her favourite is jelly.
Her mum makes it every day,
And she eats it at tea-time.
She loves all the flavours,
But her favourite is lime.

The Man Who Was Always Right

"Please don't argue,
Don't pick a fight."
Said the man who was always right.
"I know what I'm doing.
I've got it in sight."
Said the man who was always right.
"I know how it works,
It's only a light."
Said the man who was always right.
"You plug it in here.
You know I am right."
Were the last words uttered.
By the man that night!

The Little Elephant's Trunk

I'm a little elephant
My trunk is much too long.
I want to use it properly,
But I always get it wrong.
I try to pick up all my food.
Grass and fruit and hay.
When it gets close to my mouth,
My trunk begins to sway.
It waves around all over the place.
Then it hits me in the face.
I get so cross, when my food falls.
Then I hear my mother's calls.
"Have you eaten all your lunch?
Come and shelter by the trees.
It's much too hot for you out there."
"But Mum." I say. "Oh please,
I haven't eaten anything,
My trunk it just won't work.
I try to hold it steady,
but it begins to jerk."

Mum says, "Come in to the shade
And I will show you just
How easily your trunk will move,
But concentrate you must.
Pick up one piece at a time
And curl your trunk like so.
Take it slowly, take it steady,
Do it really slow.
You soon will get the hang of it
And before very long,
You'll think your trunk is perfect
And you won't get it wrong."
I'm a little elephant,
My trunk is not too long.
I can use it properly,
I never get it wrong.

A Transvestite Woke Up

A transvestite woke up one morning,
And decided who he would be.
He put on tights, twin set and pearls.
And spent all that day as Lesley.

Night time came and he went to the pub.
To meet with his mates, so you see.
He pulled on slacks, pullover and tie.
And spent all that night as Leslie.

A Positive Ending

We Are In Touch

We are now in touch,
Bless the internet.
We are now in touch,
And hopefully it will let,
Us both keep in contact,
Me and my grandsons' mother.
It was she who made the first move,
For one reason or another.
But the boys don't want to see me,
I might involve their Dad.
But cards and emails I can send,
For which I am so glad.
Small moves to be taken.
Just one step at a time.
First the card, then a letter,
And somewhere down the line.
They will want to see me.
They will change their mind.
I can't wait for that day,
So I can forget the past.
When they come to see me.
When they come at last.

Lucy Green lives in the West Country with her husband and little dog. She has had several articles and poems published, but this is her first book. Hopefully, there will be many more poems and stories in years to come.

If you would like to pass on any comments to Lucy, you are welcome to contact her on:

Lucyspoems24@yahoo.com